Joyce was outstanding... an ex
Great Practical Experien. .... *......... ...uuer...*
Perfect Content and Pace... It was inspiring!

The Total You Conference has changed my life. It has catapulted
me into my next level. Since attending my first conference
I have been able to change my posture into being the woman
on the outside that I've always seen on the inside.
—J. Wright-Middleton

....There I sat one night, thinking to myself about change and how I so
desperately needed it in my life. I didn't exactly know where to begin,
but I knew that the time had come for me to start moving along a
different path. So I went downstairs and turned on the TV and there
sat Joyce Dungee Proctor, discussing the importance of networking,
and "removing the limits" from your life. I became so inspired that I
decided to attend one of her seminars. Needless to say,
I was absolutely astounded by her presence and how her message hit so
close to home for me. Joyce is an awesome and gifted motivator
who demonstrates an ability to connect to her audience on so many
levels. She inspires, encourages and challenges each and every one
of us to rise, like a phoenix from the ashes, and to "remove the
limits" from our lives that have kept us from reaching our
true calling, gifting and ultimate happiness!
—Sandra Williams

Joyce, I cannot begin to tell you how much your conference empowered me. The severance time was the best time in my life and it allowed me to have a closer relationship with God, not to mention it allowed me to self reflect. Now that Joyce, was quite an experience. It allowed me to go inward and realize alot of my insecurities and the many masks I wore as well as allowing things and people to define who I was. I can say you have helped me with that and continue to help me with it. You are truly a divine connection to all that you come in contact with.

—RENEE CUFFIE WILLIAMS

Joyce Dungee Proctor is the truth! When she walks into a room, her mere presence brings about an energy that is exhilarating! Her seminar, Take the Limits Off, has inspired many people, including me, to step out on faith and take the necessary steps to fulfill our dreams, whatever the dream may be. This book is an opportunity for her to reach a much broader audience and share her expertise. Not only will Joyce inspire you, she will also empower you with the necessary tools to achieve greatness.

—REGINA G. GRAHAM, PRESIDENT & CEO
GRAHAM EVENT MANAGEMENT SERVICES, LLC

When I first heard Joyce speak, her words of truth and inspiration touched something deep inside of me. Joyce's take-charge message and fearless example encouraged me to reach those "unreachable places" in my own life. I always get emotional at her events, because I honestly feel the release as I apply her techniques. That's why I keep coming back.

—HANIFA SHABAZZ, CITY COUNCIL - 4TH DISTRICT
WILMINGTON, DELAWARE

SERIES ONE

TAKE *the* LIMITS OFF

SERIES ONE

TAKE
the
LIMITS
OFF

Nine Ways to Stop Talking

and Start Doing

JOYCE DUNGEE PROCTOR

ISBN: 978-0-9825594-0-6

By phone:
302-438-8478

By e-mail:
Joyce@SeminarsByJoyce.com

By mail:
Seminars by Joyce - The Total You, Inc.
P.O. Box 26183
Wilmington, DE 19899
On the World Wide Web:
www.SeminarsByJoyce.com

Cover Design:
Kita Williams, Brand [U] Inc.
www.branduinc.com

DEDICATION

This book is dedicated to the four most important people in my life, whom I love without limits. The first is my mother, the late Lucille Dungee, who carried me for the first nine months of my life and then supported me emotionally every day thereafter until she went home to be with the Lord. The second is my father, Arthur A. Dungee, a loving source of encouragement, strength, joy and love. The third is my husband, Vernell F. Proctor, Jr., the love of my life and the rock upon whom I have relied for thirty-one years. The fourth is my son, Vernell F. Proctor III, my miracle baby whom I carried for nine months, seven of which were on bed rest. I know he will carry the values of *Take The Limits Off* into his life and into the lives of many others.

In addition, I'd like to dedicate this book to my amazing, wonderful, supportive, loving, and supremely dedicated Dream Team, each of whom has supported me unconditionally. You know who you are. Thank you. I love you.

Through faith, all things are possible.

TABLE OF CONTENTS

TABLE OF CONTENTS *(continued)*

PART III: *Execute!*

ACKNOWLEDGMENTS

My gratitude for help on this project goes out to my editor, Brandon Yusuf Toropov of iWordSmith.com; to my brand designer Kita Williams of Brand [U] Inc. Finally, I am deeply grateful to Pastor Jerome Lewis of Seeds of Greatness Bible Church for the Faith teachings he has shared with me. It was at his church that I discovered how to take the limits off!

Prologue:

WHY I WROTE THIS BOOK

I wrote this book to encourage, inspire and motivate you to **Take The Limits Off.**

My goal is to share some tools that will help you to pursue your life's purpose and fulfill your dreams – tools that have worked well for me, and that I believe can work just as well for you.

Like most of the people I work with, I spent a lot of my life dreaming, wishing and hoping. My inner dialogue sounded like this:

No Limits!

This book shares proven tools for pursuing your life's purpose and fulfilling your personal dreams.

1

If only I could ...

One day, I will ...

When I save enough money, I will...

When I have the support, I will ...

When my luck changes, I will ...

When I get my degree, I will ...

When the children grow up, I will ...

...and, on and on it went ... until one day I ran into this special gift called Faith.

I had heard of Faith before, but never really grabbed hold of it. As you will see in the pages that follow, there came a point in my life when I grabbed hold of Faith with both hands. When that happened, either I would not let Faith go, or Faith would not let go of me – but regardless of which it was, I started to believe like never before.

No Limits!

This journey we are on is not about where we are from ... it is all about where we are going.

I started to think differently, speak differently, and act differently. I saw life through another lens. I saw myself changing before my own eyes. I began living in terms of possibilities.

Suddenly, the internal dialogue changed. I had a mission. I had to let the world know that this journey we are on is not about where we are from ... it is all about where we are going.

Life happens in seasons and I guess that's when I found myself in a new season called Faith! It was then that I grabbed on to Faith with both hands and learned a major lesson; that I must be open to unlimited possibilities.

As a result of learning that lesson, my life was suddenly better than it had ever been before. I was no longer a spectator. I was now in the game—the game of LIFE! I had finally stopped talking ... and started doing. My prayer for you as we begin this journey together is that what you find in these pages will help you to grab hold of Faith with both hands ... and get in the game.

Let's get started!

Part One

Create the Possibilities

Step One:

GIVE YOURSELF PERMISSION TO DREAM BIG

*H*ave you ever had a passion for something that you could almost feel and taste?

Maybe there came a moment when you tried to share this wonderful passion with someone else...and that person proceeded to tell you all the reasons why it was impossible for you to achieve all the things you had in mind...or any of them. The moment you began listening to that person, and stopped listening to your own passion, you revoked your own permission to dream big. *The other person didn't do it to you. You did it to yourself.*

Maybe you thought about leaving your corporate career to start your own business, and someone you respected quickly told you:

"You are nuts even to think about this. Don't do it." If the person urged you to stop dreaming, and you accepted that invitation, you have only yourself to hold accountable. *The other person didn't take away permission for you to dream big. You withdrew it all by yourself.*

Maybe you had a dream to break into the music industry, start your own clothing line, open your own salon or write another great American novel. As hard as you tried to explain to others that this was your passion, they just couldn't see it.

It's okay for them not to see it.

It was given to *you.*

That dream was placed on the inside of *you.* That's why *you* light up when you think about it, talk about it and dream about it. Remember this the next time you try to explain your vision to someone else. They're not bad people for not understanding your dream. They haven't experienced that dream with the same intensity that you have. Let them say whatever they want...but *MAKE YOUR OWN DECISIONS ABOUT YOUR OWN DREAMS.*

Give yourself permission to stop talking and start doing. Right now. Today. Some of the people you know may not have fulfilled *their* dreams. That is no excuse for you to stop trying, or stop dreaming, or stop planning.

No Limits!

"Practical dreamers never quit."

NAPOLEON HILL

Give yourself permission to dream big...in full color... without limitations! If you could do, go, or become anything that you desired, what kind of person would you become? Where would you go? What would you do? How would you start?

What if you made a habit of daydreaming about your dream? What if you could visualize it so clearly that you could feel it, touch it, believe it ... and actually build that dream? What if it were *you* who had the power to give yourself permission to dream big, and achieve big things?

Go find a mirror, right now, and look into it for thirty seconds. Then, come back to this page.

The person you were just looking at is the *one* human being on this earth with the greatest control over your happiness, success, fulfillment, and well-being.

It is you who will make the difference in your life!

You must feel so passionate about your dream that you become unstoppable: someone

No Limits!

It is you who will make the difference in your life!

who is on a mission. In service of that mission, you will engage with others, side-step obstacles, kick down doors, smash through road blocks, leap over walls, and take any other appropriate actions to move your mission forward; all because of your inspired passion and determination.

Once you give yourself permission to dream, move forward just because you choose to. Yes, choose to exercise your power of choice. That's the power that lies within you! Make the choice today and give yourself a GIFT that is long overdue. Grant yourself permission to THINK BIG!

There is no time like the present to give yourself this permission.

Giving yourself permission to dream big is the key to uncovering the greatness that is on the inside of you. This is what will spur you to stop talking and start doing!

It was only by granting myself this permission to dream, and then pursuing that motivating dream through faith and action, that I was able to move forward to a place of fulfillment, joy, and true love in my life. Because I gave myself permission to dream big, I discovered what I was born to do. Once I had discovered it, I could pursue it – and achieve it. You, too, can experience this remarkable self-awakening...*if you are willing to begin at the beginning and dream your own dreams – big.* This is the critical step. This is the beginning of the journey. I wrote this book so that you and I could take the journey together.

Once you start dreaming big, anything is possible. Once I gave myself permission to dream big, everyone began to assume that I had it going on! This was because that seemingly minor, internal change made a big difference in the way I presented myself to the world. It also made a big difference in the way I was treated by other people – including some of the people who had told me that I was "nuts" for dreaming in the first place! People started treating me with more respect *once I began treating my own dream with respect.* When this first started happening, I thought to myself, "Little do they know that I'm a work in progress, like everyone else!"

Then it dawned on me. **We are all a work in progress.**

* * *

"Dream as if you'll live forever, live as if you'll die today."
—JAMES DEAN

"You see things; and you say, 'Why?'
But I dream things that never were; and I say, 'Why not?'"
—GEORGE BERNARD SHAW

"Keep your dreams alive. Understand to achieve anything requires
faith and belief in yourself, vision, hard work, determination, and
dedication. Remember all things are possible for those who believe."
—GAIL DEVERS

WORKSHEET: DREAM BIG

For one minute, go back to a time or a point in your life when you achieved a goal or dream that meant a great deal to you. What did it feel like to achieve what you wanted? How did you do it? What rewards came your way? How could you do something like that again?

Once you have silently answered these questions to your own satisfaction, and *not before,* complete the following sentence:

IF I COULD DO ABSOLUTELY ANYTHING TODAY, AND HAD NO LIMITATIONS WHATSOEVER IN MY LIFE, I WOULD...

Step Two:

Spend Time With Yourself

*Y*ou can uncover great things about who you are, what you want to do, and what you are capable of, just by spending a little time with yourself each and every day.

Go ahead. It's okay to have one-on-one personal time with yourself. Try it! I know you will enjoy some "me" time. Make time to recline, relax, and reflect. Schedule an appointment with yourself. It will be the most important appointment of the day.

This may be hard for some of us to do with our busy schedules, but we should begin anyway by admitting that we owe this to ourselves. We do ... and we must find a way to pay ourselves what we owe.

I never would have moved forward and launched my company if I hadn't decided to spend time with myself.

For years, I had been speaking as part of my day job, and for fun—but it never occurred to me to try to speak professionally until someone approached me after one of my events and asked me, "How much do you charge?"

That question had never, ever crossed my mind before, and I said as much. The man who approached me smiled and said, "Well, you're very good. You should consider doing this full time. If you ever decide to do this professionally, I hope you'll give me a call." He handed me his business card.

That moment changed my life. It started me thinking. I began meditating, soul-searching, exploring: Should I be speaking professionally? Did I have the internal resources necessary to do this? Was I in the right season in my life to pull something like this off? Instead of simply brushing those questions aside, I made a commitment to spend a few hours a week with them.

I started taking time, every morning, to be quiet and still enough to address those questions. For a half an hour each morning, I took some quiet time to myself and started writing the best questions I could, followed by the best answers I could.

Did I speak well enough? Who would I speak to? Who would support me – a little girl from the projects? For years, I had been shy and afraid to speak in public. Was this really possible for me?

I was afraid! Please hear me loud and clear: I mean *afraid*. Every morning, I would meditate and pray for guidance on how I could overcome my fears and be the very best I could be. Every time

I looked around at the other wonderful professional speakers out there, I thought, "I could never do that!"

In the mornings, when I was spending time with myself, I would hear a little voice talking back to me: "Or could I?"

I came to recognize the "I couldn't possibly do that" message for what it was: A self-limiting belief. I prayed for guidance every day, so I could get past that self-limiting belief. And it worked.

I'm here to tell you that, whatever it is you're now telling yourself that you love doing, but think you "can't" do at the level of excellence you desire— you *can* do it! Use time on your own to learn how to stop playing the negative background music. Use that time to change the station, or turn the radio off completely.

Here's the paradox. By spending time with myself, I learned how to take the focus *off* of myself. I discovered that what I was doing was not about me; it was about serving others. My whole life's journey had been all about preparation for this very moment in my life. Everything I needed was already on the inside of me. It was now time for me to nurture and improve my gifts, talents and strengths, so I could improve my world and thereby bring out the best in the people that I deal with daily.

No Limits!

By learning to spend time with yourself, you learn to take the focus off of yourself.

By spending time with myself each day, I realized that my message was really for someone else! My job was to change, inspire and empower others – using my own story. We all have a story to tell. What's yours?

I began using my personal time to get everything I wanted to do, and all my plans for getting them done, down on paper. That's what made all the difference. After just a few weeks of making the investment in cultivating my dream, I became convinced that after years of supporting other people's dreams behind the scenes, that it was time for me to do what I was born to do: Step out on stage! That's how I moved from being afraid to speak in public to being afraid not to. It became apparent that speaking to help others was my duty, my mission.

No Limits!

What talents, skills and passions can you uncover by spending time with yourself each day?

What's your duty? What's your mission? If you do not use your gifts and talents in support of what you were "born to do" you will surely lose those gifts.

What gifts and talents can you uncover during your one-on-one time with yourself? What are you really great at that you are not yet pursuing?

IN ORDER TO INVEST IN YOURSELF ....

+ Could you take ten minutes of private time for yourself, starting tomorrow morning?

+ Could you make sure there are absolutely no interruptions from other people—no phone calls, no e-mails, no Internet conversations – during that period?

+ Could you continue that time commitment for at least twenty-one days?

✦ During that private time, could you pose this question—
"What was I born to do?"—and see what answer comes back?

✦ Continue the process by asking these questions: "What
am I passionate about?" "What do I love to do in my spare
time?" "What would I do for free?"

✦ "What do I do for fun? As a hobby? In my spare time?" Is it
cooking, baking, teaching, writing, drawing, singing, dancing? What is it?

✦ "What do others say I'm good at? What do I do with little
or no effort right now?"

✦ During your private time, could you spend a few minutes
each day writing about what you want to make happen next
in your life, what resources you could bring to bear, and
what kind of person you would like to see when you look
into the mirror one year from today? I remember one very
special lady came up to me after my first conference and
said, "Just think where you will be three years from now!"
That was 2006, and I did not fully understand her words at
the time – but I do now. Thank you, Lisa!

*"By three methods we may learn wisdom: first, by reflection, which
is noblest; second, by imitation, which is easiest; and third, by
experience, which is the most bitter."*
—Confucius

"Sweep before your own door first"
—Anonymous

"Follow effective action with quiet reflection.
From the quiet reflection will come even more effective action."
—PETER F. DRUCKER

WORKSHEET: SPEND TIME WITH YOURSELF

I commit to spend _____ minutes with myself each and every day, commencing at _____ am/pm.

I will honor this commitment,

Signed: _____

Date: _____

Note: If you are really serious about this commitment, get your Accountability Partner to sign, too! (See Step Eight.)

Step Three:

IDENTIFY YOUR GOAL AND DREAM

I now believed in myself enough to know that I needed a goal to formalize the direction in which I was moving. After spending all that time on my own, my number one goal—the definite chief purpose of my life—became clear to me. I wanted to start my own speaking career ... and be compensated for it. Could I really get paid for doing what I loved? By setting that goal for myself, I was answering that question with a single word: YES.

I knew what I had to do: Start creating and delivering programs that could inspire people.

I began researching the speaking industry inside and out. I did this on the side, in my off hours, while still holding down a full-time job. It occured to me that I could use my full-time job to support my larger goal. (You probably can, too.)

No Limits!

A goal is the answer to the question, "What am I most excited about accomplishing, and by when do I want to accomplish it?"

Then came the hard part of setting my fee structure, being consistent in charging the fee and charging the appropriate fee for each seminar booked. This is a challenge when you love what you do and have done it for free for so long. Nevertheless, you must pass the same test I passed, and attach a clear dollar value to the product or service you are offering.

A goal is the answer to the question, "What am I most excited about accomplishing, and by when do I want to accomplish it?" After a good deal of thought, I wrote my goal down on a piece of paper. Here's what it looked like:

Set fees for seminars, keynote speeches and workshops; be consistent; target one booking per week for the next 90 days.

There were also some intermediate goals I set up along the way, sub-goals that supported the main goals I had set up for myself. Here's what they looked like:

Conduct information gathering/research speaking fees with meeting planners

**Schedule time to speak with other professional speakers,
one per week for at least four weeks**

Target contacts in my network to schedule one on one meetings

**Prepare a list of questions I have and challenges I face—and
spend some time identifying how I would get the answers and
meet the challenges head on**

Just reviewing this list, I am reminded of all the new people I met along the way, people who helped me by sharing their knowledge and making room for someone new. I am so grateful for their help! Your own allies are waiting for you to discover them. *But you must have a clear goal if you expect to attract them to you.*

By writing down my goal, by getting specific about it, by getting excited about it, and by creating sub-goals that supported it, I began the all-important process of OWNING that goal ...of making it truly mine. You can, too.

I became more and more invested in my goal by reviewing it each and every day—and by reminding myself of the importance that historical figures I admired most had placed on goals and goal-setting. Here are some of the quotes that have made a difference to me, and may make a difference to you:

*"Only those who will risk going too far can possibly find out
how far one can go. "*
~ T. S. ELIOT

"Obstacles are those frightful things you see when you take your eyes off your goal."

~ HENRY FORD

"If you aim at nothing, you'll hit it every time."

~ UNKNOWN

"The greater danger for most of us is not that our aim is too high and we miss it, but that it is too low and we hit it."

~ MICHELANGELO

"Give me a stock clerk with a goal and I'll give you a man who will make history. Give me a man with no goals and I'll give you a stock clerk."

~ J.C. PENNEY

"What you get by achieving your goals is not as important as what you become by achieving your goals."

~ ZIG ZIGLAR

"If you don't know where you're going, you're likely to end up someplace else."

~YOGI BERRA

WORKSHEET: "SMART" GOALS

You must have a definite goal, and you must own that goal! This worksheet will help. In the space below, write down your DEFINITE CHIEF AIM IN LIFE.

_____

_____

_____

_____

_____

_____

_____

_____

_____

_____

_____

_____

_____

_____

_____

Now, check your goals against the following criteria:

+ Is the goal Specific? (Will you know when you've attained it? How?)
+ Is the goal Measurable? (Are there clear benchmarks along the way?)
+ Is the goal Achievable? (Is it a bit of a stretch—but within your grasp?)
+ Is the goal Realistic? (Have you got a role model—living or dead—who accomplished something similar?)
+ Is there a Timetable? (What is the clear, specific date by which you will have attained this goal?)

If the goal you've written down doesn't meet all five of these criteria—revise it until it does!

Note: If you are really serious about this goal ... share it with your Accountability Partner! (See Step Eight.)

Section Notes

Section Notes

Section Notes

Section Notes

Part Two

Get Unstuck

Step Four:

IDENTIFY YOUR LIMITATIONS

*N*ow, I was really excited about the prospect of starting my own business! It seemed like I was poised to take off.

The trouble was, my plane wasn't yet ready to leave the runway. I didn't expect to hit an obstacle right away ... but that's what happened. Every time I got myself into a position where I was about to take action, it seemed like a hundred fears, negative thoughts, and skeptical questions began crowding into my mind all over again. Here's what they sounded like:

I'm not good enough!

What makes me think I have the resources I need to do this?

What makes me think I have the experience I need to do this?

Who in the world is going to pay to hear me speak about anything?

What happens if ... (here I would play out
some terrible scenario for myself)

On and on it went. My head wouldn't stop spinning. These were all examples of self-inflicted fears and doubts: obstacles that I put up for myself. I realized that I was bringing "negative background music" into my own life. And I was pretty good at it. After all, I had been doing it for years!

STEP FOUR is where you identify exactly what has stopped you in the past from taking action on your goals.

No Limits!

Identify exactly what has stopped you in the past from taking action on your goals.

In my case (and perhaps in yours, too) the obstacle was self-inflicted fears and doubts. To overcome this obstacle, I had to activate my own personal faith in a big way. I had to make a conscious choice to put in plenty of "good stuff" to counteract all the "bad stuff" that I had become accustomed to telling myself. I had to tune in to what was stopping me–irrational self-limiting fears and negative thoughts–and I had to get clear enough about what was happening to actually be aware of it, each and every time it did happen.

If you don't remain aware of what has held you back in the past and take the appropriate action to remove that obstacle now; how can you expect to move forward in the future?

In my case, I changed the equation, and overcame the obstacle, by changing what I was actually putting into my head. I bombarded myself with positive messages, in the form of books, audio programs, and articles. I changed the way I looked at my life goals. I started changing my internal language. Instead of asking myself what could go wrong, I started explaining to myself "what could go right" in any given situation. Instead of thinking about what I "wanted" to do, I started thinking in terms of my "duty" to deliver positive results to others through my talks and seminars. I began thinking about this as my calling—and actually I got to the point where I was afraid *not* to take action.

Before I could make any of those things happen, however, I had to know what was actually keeping me from moving forward to take action on my goals. I figured out what was stopping me, and I learned to notice it and counteract it every time it appeared in my life.

What's stopping you?

"He who would be useful, strong, and happy must cease to be a passive receptacle for the negative, beggarly, and impure streams of thought; and as a wise householder commands his servants and invites his guests, so must he learn to command his desires and to say, with authority, what thoughts he shall admit into the mansion of his soul."

—JAMES ALLEN

"Setting a goal is not the main thing. It is deciding how you will go about achieving it and then staying with that plan."

—TOM LANDRY

"Four steps to achievement: Plan purposefully. Prepare prayerfully. Proceed positively. Pursue persistently."

—WILLIAM A. WARD

WORKSHEET: WHAT'S STOPPING YOU?

Things that have stopped me in the past include:

_____

_____

_____

_____

_____

_____

_____

_____

_____

_____

_____

_____

_____

_____

_____

_____

_____

_____

Step Five:

Conduct a SWOT Analysis

*O*nce you know your goal, and identify what has stopped you in the past, do an in depth analysis of your STRENGTHS, WEAKNESSES, OPPORTUNITIES, and THREATS as they relate to your goal.

As I set out to start my business, my major STRENGTH was the relationships I had that I could rely on for resources and support.

My major WEAKNESS was that I had a lot of ideas in my head, but I had not yet put them down on paper. As a result, I was not yet holding myself accountable for important actions.

I discovered that my chief OPPORTUNITIES were the many people and groups who could benefit from hearing my message.

A major THREAT I faced was my own lack of market knowledge. I still needed to educate myself.

No Limits!

Once you know your goal, do an in depth analysis of your STRENGTHS, WEAKNESSES, OPPORTUNITIES, and THREATS as they relate to that goal.

This kind of self-analysis is an ongoing process—a personal review I now conduct about once a month. You should do the same kind of self-analysis.

Let's look more closely at each of these elements.

One of the things I realized from conducting my own SWOT analysis was that, in order to move forward on my goal, I had to have a much deeper understanding of my own natural strengths. These included relationship building, leadership, communication, and my own positive attitude. I encourage you to list yours on a piece of paper and then post them where you can easily see them each and every day.

These were things I loved doing, was good at doing, and didn't have to think twice about. They were things people had always praised me for doing. I learned to build the value I delivered to people around these strengths.

I also found weaknesses—not challenges, but weaknesses. These were areas where I knew I didn't perform well, areas where I knew I would need help from other people. I realized that I *could not* build the value I delivered to people around these weaknesses!

The opportunities were resources I already had that related to my goal. This was an extremely important category because there were a lot of resources that I didn't know I had. The market for my services was far larger than I expected; and so was the number of people willing to help me reach my goal!

The threats, of course, were the things that stood in my way or had the danger of taking me off track. Many of them connected to my weaknesses. Dropping back into my fear mindset was always a big threat I had to deal with, but there were (and are) plenty of external obstacles, as well.

Whatever your goal is ... IT'S NOT REALLY A GOAL UNTIL YOU'RE PREPARED TO CONDUCT A MONTHLY SWOT ANALYSIS IN SUPPORT OF IT!

"It takes as much energy to wish as it does to plan."

—ELEANOR ROOSEVELT

"You can change your beliefs so they empower your dreams and desires. Create a strong belief in yourself and what you want."

—LES BROWN

*"I have given myself the permission to do what
I enjoy—and enjoy what I do."*

—BILL GATES

WORKSHEET: YOUR SWOT ANALYSIS

✦ STRENGTHS: What are you good at right now? What do others say you do well?

✦ WEAKNESSES: What needs improving? What are others likely to consider your "Achilles Heel"?

✦ OPPORTUNITIES: What are the very best opportunities in front of you right now? Which connect most closely to your strengths?

✦ THREATS: What could harm you, either in the short term or the long term? Where do your weaknesses leave you most vulnerable?

Step Six:

MANAGE THE FOUR TYPES OF PEOPLE

*O*nce you get this far, an extremely important factor comes into play: Your social circle. This factor is so important that it's the subject of two separate chapters in this book.

Some people try to pretend that the people they choose to spend their time with don't really affect their goal orientation or their mission in life. They try to tell themselves that they alone control their emotions, their focus, and their capacity to take action ... but they're wrong.

If you doubt the importance of your social circle, let me ask you a question. Suppose you could choose the people your children's teacher spent time with, and you could choose anyone on earth—

whom would you choose? Most parents say things like "world leaders" or "Nobel Laureates." We don't have any proof that the teacher who spends all of her available free time hanging out with the Nobel prize winners will necessarily be better at her job than the one who spends her time with people picked at random from the phone book ... but we assume that she does, right? Why is that?

No Limits!

Birds of a feather really do flock together. What kind of bird do you want to be?

It's because birds of a feather really do flock together. If you expect to turn your goals into reality, you have to start making some conscious choices about the types of birds you decide to flock with. I discovered, from personal experience, that they fall into four main categories, as follows:

+ DREAM STEALERS. These are people who resent it when other people succeed, including you. They're only happy when they can see themselves as the most important or successful person in the room. Unfortunately, we all run into our share of these birds, and sometimes we even end up working for them full time. That doesn't mean we have to FLOCK with them, though. Your social circle, of course, consists of the people you choose to spend time with. Right now, identify one person in your life experience, from your present or your past, who qualifies as a DREAM STEALER. Then ask yourself: How much time am I spending with this person?

+ NAYSAYERS; These are actually the opposite of the DREAM STEALERS. They want to make sure every one is just as unsuccessful and unhappy as they are, so they'll take every opportunity to tell (supposed) friends and loved ones why aiming high in life is a bad idea. Can you think of anyone like this from your own experience? I thought so. Now ask yourself: How much time am I currently spending with this person?

+ BACK STABBERS: These birds are among the scariest. As the old song goes, "they smile in your face" ... but when you're not around, they're working against you and trying to talk you down. They will work behind the scenes to keep you from attaining your goals and keep you from becoming the best person you can. Can you think of anyone like this from your own experience? How much time are you currently spending with this person?

+ SUPPORTERS: These are people who will back your play—people who respect you for thinking big, and want to help you turn your dreams into reality. They support you—period. Who can you think of from your own experience who falls into this category? How much time are you spending with these people?

"A friend is someone who understands your past, believes in your future, and accepts you just the way you are."

—ANONYMOUS

"A friend is someone who, upon seeing another friend in immense pain, would rather be the one experiencing the pain than to have to watch their friend suffer."

—ANONYMOUS

"A true friend is someone who thinks that you are a good egg even though he knows that you are slightly cracked"

—BERNARD MELTZER

WORKSHEET: MANAGE THE FOUR TYPES OF PEOPLE

Do a quick inventory, using the form below:

✦ Last week, I spent approximately _____ % of my available social time (virtual or face to face) with DREAM STEALERS.

✦ Last week, I spent approximately _____ % of my available social time (virtual or face to face) with NAY SAYERS.

✦ Last week, I spent approximately _____ % of my available social time (virtual or face to face) with BACK-STABBERS.

✦ Last week, I spent approximately _____ % of my available social time (virtual or face to face) with SUPPORTERS.

Section Notes

Section Notes

Section Notes

Section Notes

Part Three

Execute!

Step Seven:

IDENTIFY YOUR DREAM TEAM

*W*ithin the group of supporters you just identified is a special collection of people who support your goals and dreams, and whom you support in return. These should be people who know you well, who respect your abilities, who are unfailingly optimistic, who would never, ever try to talk you into believing something disempowering about yourself, and whom you could trust with major decisions if you were unable to make those decisions for any reason.

Before you go any further in this book, think of at least SEVEN people you've got in your camp right now who match this description. Write their names and telephone numbers in the spaces below.

1. _____

2. _____

3. _____

4. _____

5. _____

6. _____

7. _____

These are the members of your DREAM TEAM. You've got to have seven of them because there are seven days in the week. Each and every day that you are above ground and drawing breath,

No Limits!

Reach out, on a daily basis, to the people you love and respect most!

you will reach out to a member of your DREAM TEAM and make either VOICE TO VOICE or FACE TO FACE contact with that person, and briefly share what you plan to do that day. (E-mail messages, Facebook postings, or similar messages don't count, though you can certainly do those in addition to what I'm describing here.) During your discussion, you will learn what is happening in that person's world.

You will now start reaching out, on a daily basis, to the people you love and respect most.

You will now start reinforcing these critical alliances.

You will now start contributing to, and drawing strength from, the DREAM TEAM that can help you brainstorm your plan, troubleshoot your plan, and, eventually, turn your plan into a reality.

You will now start spending some part of every single day in contact with people who will remind you of who you really are.

Look back at the list you've just created. If you're like most of the people I work with, you'll see that on that list is at least ONE person you haven't talked to in thirty days or more. If that's the case with your list ... stop and think about what that means for a moment. This is a critical friend and ally—someone you would literally trust with your life—and a whole month has gone by without you making personal contact!

Reach out to that person today and say, "I was just thinking of you." Then tell the person about your new goal, and about your decision to draft this person onto your DREAM TEAM—and to support that person through thick and thin.

This week, you will take action to bring seven strong, supportive people into your circle – people you trust, people with whom you have good chemistry, people with integrity who will hold you accountable to your own mission and your own commitments.

From this day forward, every day will be a day when you connect with your DREAM TEAM.

"Call it a clan, call it a network, call it a tribe, call it a family: Whatever you call it, whoever you are, you need one."

—JANE HOWARD

"The successful networkers I know, the ones receiving tons of referrals and feeling truly happy about themselves, continually put the other person's needs ahead of their own."

—BOB BURG

"More business decisions occur over lunch and dinner than at any other time, yet no MBA courses are given on the subject."

—PETER DRUCKER

WORKSHEET: IDENTIFY YOUR DREAM TEAM

Dream Team Member	Last Date Contacted	Next Date I Will Contact
_____	_____	_____
_____	_____	_____
_____	_____	_____
_____	_____	_____
_____	_____	_____
_____	_____	_____
_____	_____	_____
_____	_____	_____
_____	_____	_____
_____	_____	_____
_____	_____	_____
_____	_____	_____
_____	_____	_____
_____	_____	_____
_____	_____	_____
_____	_____	_____

Step Eight:

CREATE AN INITIAL PLAN WITH AN ACCOUNTABILITY PARTNER

*L*et's look at what we've figured out so far about the universe of people who connect to you. The diagram on the next page describes a special zone I call the Trust Circle.

Outside of the borders of the Trust Circle lie the people who, for whatever reasons, are out to make it harder for you to turn your dream into reality. They carry out their mission by finding ways to spend time with you. We've met them in a previous chapter: the

THE TRUST CIRCLE™

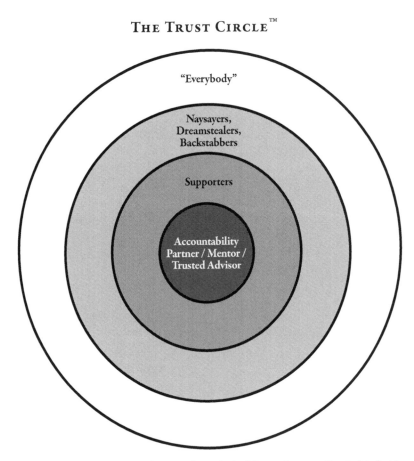

Nay Sayers, Dream Stealers, and Back Stabbers. Personally, I think it's pointless trying to figure out *why* these people do the things they do; most of the time, they don't really know for sure themselves. The point is, you can't trust them with your attention or your energy. The more time you spend with them, the greater the jeopardy will be to your dream.

Your most important challenge on any given day is probably going to be this one: *How do I spend as little time as possible (and preferably no time at all) with people who lie outside of my Trust Circle?*

In the first area of your trust circle, you will find your Allies. These are the people who are eager to see you succeed. The members of your Dream Team all lie within this outer circle. The more time, attention, and energy you give these people, the better off your dream will be.

In the center of your Trust Circle, you will create a special place for a special person. Some people call this person an ac-

No Limits!

At the center of your Trust Circle is a special kind of ally.

countability partner; others use the name Mentor or Trusted Advisor. Whatever you call this person, he or she is a special kind of ally.

This is someone who's your cheerleader, who has your best interests at heart, and with whom you can share a particular goal and the timeline you have set for yourself for attaining that goal. You want to spend as much time as possible with this person.

You may choose to put one person in this circle ... or you may be more comfortable working with multiple accountability partners, each connecting to one of your major goals. What's important is that you talk about specific goals and timelines on a regular basis with this person, and that you do so with a sense of positive expectation!

Put the goal on paper. Put the timeline on paper. Review it regularly with the person at the very center of your Trust Circle!

* * *

It was time to launch my new company website, one that I could be very proud of and that would service my clients well. I was very excited. I conducted research for weeks, had professional photos taken, and wrote all-new copy. I checked out as many websites as I possibly could. Finally, I complied all of my research and consulted with the project manager who would be overseeing the entire project. I shared my vision with her team; they embraced it as their own and created a step-by-step plan. What a blessing it is to have supportive, talented people in your camp!

Now I had an action plan to launch a quality web site, a web site that supported my overall mission. I gave myself a timeline: six months. I put my trusted adviser, the project manager, who was a gifted web site designer, at the center of my Trust Circle—not for every goal in my life, but for this particular goal. I was able to paint a picture for her of exactly what I intended to accomplish; we collaborated on the timeline, and we made adjustments along the way. We also *celebrated* along the way, which is something I'll be discussing in more depth in the Epilogue of this book. Each time we hit one of our milestones, we found some way to reward ourselves for all of the hard work that had made it possible for us to move a little further toward the finish line!

That project manager wasn't just a "vendor" to me—she was a TRUSTED ADVISOR who occupied the very center of my Trust Circle! Thanks to her, we completed that web site before six months had elapsed, and today it is the keystone of my business. We are incredibly proud of it! (You can take a look for yourself by visiting www.seminarsbyjoyce.com.)

You don't have to be good in order to start, but you and your Accountability Partner must definitely *start* if you want to be good!

* * *

*"If you think you can, you can. And if you think
you can't, you're right."*

—MARY KAY ASH

"Accountability is not a result; it's your competitive advantage."

—SAM SILVERSTEIN

*"If a man coaches himself, then he has only himself
to blame when he is beaten."*

—ROGER BANNISTER

WORKSHEET: TAKE ACTION!

Your Accountability Partner must be someone who believes in your goal, who has accomplished their goals and can hold you to your commitment to yourself for accomplishing yours. This person may need to implement a "tough love" plan. Choose this person carefully. Once you have identified someone you think is your Accountability Partner, ask yourself these questions.

1. Has this person already achieved notable success that is directly related to his or her specific personal goals?

2. Would I trust this person with a major life decision?

3. Will this person make time for me?

4. Am I comfortable working with this person?

5. If I ask this person to implement "tough love" when it comes to holding me accountable for a goal, will he or she do that?

Step Nine:

BENCHMARK IT!

𝒾n any project that's important to you, you must set up benchmarks that will confirm measurable progress along the way toward the goal. Measure and evaluate your progress toward that goal, then discuss and critique your progress with your Accountability Partner on a regular basis. If necessary, you must alter your approach in order to make measurable progress. Sometimes, you must be willing to adopt new ideas that come from people who have more experience than you do and are willing to share their insights and advice.

I realize that the word "benchmarking" covers a lot of ground. Let me give you a clear example of what I'm talking about, an example that will demonstrate the vital importance of having a clear target and regular discussion sessions to evaluate your progress toward that target.

In 2007, I attended a conference in Philadelphia, Pennsylvania. I was scheduled to meet a co-worker there at 9:00 am in the lobby. I was not feeling very well, and I arrived late. My co-worker was no longer in the lobby; she was in a seminar , but I could not manage to locate her. I walked from seminar to seminar, looking for a topic that would interest me. Finally I came to a door where I heard a wonderful speaker by the name of Pegine Echevarria presenting her ideas with joy, laughter, hope and enthusiasm, I could not walk away. I knew that this was the topic for me! I stepped in and took in her program. After the seminar, I purchased a copy of Pegine's book. I thought, "Wow! This is great; all of the speakers are selling their books at these events." I began to chat with the speaker, told her how much I had enjoyed her program, and asked her for advice on writing and publishing a book. (This was one of my major goals, but so far, I had not made much measurable progress toward attaining the goal.) Instantly, she gave me the contact information for her editor!

No Limits!

If you don't know how, you'd better ask somebody who does.

MY BENCHMARKING PHILOSOPHY: If you don't know how, you'd better ask somebody who does.

So it was then that I began work with a professional editor to create a series of articles and, eventually, this book.

Once we started working on the book project, I told my editor exactly what my message was, what I wanted to accomplish with the book, and when I wanted to be ready to send the book to the printer. Working together, we set up a table of contents that laid out the book's structure, and we identified the nine central chapters that supported my message. We then set up a series of conference calls. I developed materials that supported each of the nine steps we had identified, and I passed what I had along to my editor. We discussed and refined the material as part of our regular series of calls, and we traded the files back and forth. All the way through, we were adjusting our approach to the content, and measuring our progress on the nine main chapters against the target completion date we had set for ourselves. The result is the book that you are now holding in your hands.

I call what I was doing—when I reached out to someone with experience, adopted a new set of tactics, revised my goal's targets, and kept measuring my progress—BENCHMARKING. That speaker knew more about finishing a book than I did. The editor and I set up, and revised, a plan with clear targets that allowed us to measure exactly how close we were to reaching the goal. Together, we worked toward that target, and discussed our progress along the way.

According to 12Manage.com, there are five distinct kinds of benchmarking:

+ INTERNAL: You and an ally set the intermediate targets based on your own experience and insights, you discuss your progress toward those targets, and you work toward them together. (This is what my editor and I were doing.)

✦ COMPETITIVE: You monitor the competition for processes, and set targets that model their process.

✦ FUNCTIONAL: You find something similar that a non-competitor is doing in your industry, and set targets that model that process.

✦ GENERIC: You find something similar that a non-competitor is doing in a different industry, and set targets that model that process.

✦ COLLABORATIVE: You find multiple partners working in a wide variety of different settings, and use the diversity of the group's experience to set targets and critique progress toward them.

If you can't measure it ... it's not benchmarking.

If you can't break it into discrete parts .. it's not benchmarking.

If you can't schedule it ... it's not benchmarking.

If you can't discuss it along the way ... it's not benchmarking.

* * *

"Benchmarking is a reference point that is used as a comparison to everything that follows."

—BERNARD WALTERS

"If you know the enemy and know yourself, you need not fear the result of a hundred battles."

—SUN TZU

"Our goals can only be reached through a vehicle of a plan, in which we must fervently believe, and upon which we must vigorously act. There is no other route to success."

—STEPHEN A. BRENNAN

WORKSHEET: REVISE THE PLAN AND BENCHMARK IT!

Ask yourself:

+ How am I currently measuring progress toward this goal?
+ Should I be measuring it differently?
+ Am I on track? If so, why? If not, why not?
+ Has anything important changed since I set this goal?
+ Is this still the right goal for me?
+ What are the main elements of my plan to achieve this goal?
+ Am I actually following this plan? If not, why not?
+ Do I need to change the plan?
+ Who have I reached out to for support and guidance in attaining this goal? What good ideas from that person have I incorporated into my plan?
+ What resources do I need if I am going to attain this goal?
+ What's working about the way I am moving toward this goal?
+ What's not working?
+ Have I been ethical and honest in pursuit of this goal? Would I be content if everything I did or said to attain this goal showed up on the front page of the *New York Times* tomorrow morning?
+ Am I enjoying the process of moving toward the fulfillment of this goal? If not, am I at least positively anticipating the end result?

Section Notes

Section Notes

Section Notes

Section Notes

Epilogue:

CELEBRATE AND FORGIVE

You must celebrate every victory, be it large or small, that you experience along the way to your goal. My own experience in training people in these principles is that celebration is the part of the process that "busy" people are most likely to overlook. This is a major issue, because the act of celebrating puts your mind in a position of GRATITUDE ... and cultivating an awareness of the many things in life that you have reason to be grateful for is essential to your success. If you are too busy to celebrate milestones along the way to achieving your goal, then YOU ARE TOO BUSY, PERIOD!

When I was working with my web designer to upgrade my site, I made a point of finding ways to celebrate all the little milestones along the way: the selection of the theme colors, the creation of the right photograph, the creation of the first rough design for the home page. Our celebrations took the form of simple gifts we shared, or of e-cards, or even a personalized note explaining how grateful I was for all the work that had taken place thus far.

The key word here is GRATITUDE. If your efforts at celebration are making you feel grateful for the many blessings you have received in your life—the air you breathe, the family members you love, the allies who are supporting you every step of the way—then you will know that you are executing this step correctly. If you are not feeling grateful, you will know you need to find new reasons to keep celebrating.

THE PEAR TREE

There was once a man who had four sons. He wanted his sons to learn not to judge things too quickly. So he sent them each on a quest, in turn, to go and look at a pear tree that was a great distance away.

The first son went in the winter, the second in the spring, the third in summer, and the youngest son in the fall. When they had all gone and come back, he called them together to describe what they had seen.

The first son said, "The tree was ugly, bent, and twisted." The second son said, "No, it was covered with green buds and full of promise." The third son disagreed; he said, "It was laden with blossoms that smelled so sweet and looked so beautiful, it was the most graceful thing I have ever seen." The last son disagreed with all of them; he said "It was ripe and drooping with fruit, full of life and fulfillment."

The man then explained to his sons that they were all right, because they had each seen but only one season in the tree's life. He told them that you cannot judge a tree, or a person, by only one season, and that the essence of who they are and the pleasure, joy, and love that come from that life can only be measured at the end, when all the seasons are up. "If you give up when it's winter, you will miss the promise of your spring, the beauty of your summer, the fulfillment of your fall."

~AUTHOR UNKNOWN

The Moral: There is often a positive side to a person or situation that we do not at first notice.

SAND AND STONE

A story tells of two friends who were walking through the desert. During some point of the journey, they had an argument, and one friend slapped the other one in the face. The one who got slapped was hurt, but without saying anything, she wrote in the sand:

"TODAY MY BEST FRIEND SLAPPED ME IN THE FACE"

They kept on walking, until they found an oasis, where they decided to take a bath. The one who had been slapped got stuck in the mire and started drowning, but her friend saved her. After she recovered from the near drowning, she wrote on a stone:

"TODAY MY BEST FRIEND SAVED MY LIFE"

The friend who had first slapped, and then saved, her best friend, asked: "After I hurt you, you wrote in the sand, and now, you write on a stone, why?"

The other friend replied: "When someone hurts us, we should write it down in sand, where the winds of forgiveness can erase it, but when someone does something good for us, we must engrave it in stone, so no wind can ever erase it."

—AUTHOR UNKNOWN

The Moral: Learn to write your hurts in the sand – and to carve your blessings in stone!

ON SOWING AND REAPING

All of the truly great figures from human history have emphasized giving, rather than receiving, as the first priority of a life well lived. All the mentors who have made a real difference in my life have placed a premium on giving and helping others (notably me). My goal now is to live up to their example ... and model the way for others.

It takes courage, discipline, and commitment to give first – but I believe it is worth it. When we give first, we sow seeds of love and possibility into the lives of others. When we give first, we begin the cycle of reciprocity and good will that makes healthy families, healthy organizations, and healthy societies possible. When we give first, we help others pass along the habit of giving first.

Chip Bell, senior partner at Performance Research Associates, tells the story of how an act of generosity transformed his life. In the summer of 1954, Bell was a young boy whose only spending money came from mowing the lawns of friends and neighbors; he received no allowance. A big lawn earned him two dollars; a small lawn earned him one dollar.

That summer, a major drought struck Georgia, and because grass doesn't grow much when rain isn't falling, Bell's lawn-mowing requests had slowed to a trickle by early July. By early August, the requests had dwindled to nothing, and the young man had no funds at all. Then came the day when his grandmother, who had a big lawn, asked if he would come over and mow it for two dollars.

The grass was short, but Bell mowed it anyway. When he was done, his grandmother handed him a five-dollar bill and said what must have been, to his ears, the sweetest words in the English language: "Keep the change."

That gesture didn't just give a boy pocket money. It eventually gave the man he grew into a legacy of generosity to remember for a lifetime – and pass along to others. "Her spirit," Bell says now, "continues to guide the choices I make about my own legacy of generosity."

Whose legacy of generosity have you benefited from in your life? Who sowed seeds that grew to make you a better person? Who gave something important to you when you needed it most? Who used a gift to save you, inspire you, and perhaps challenge you to sow seeds that would help someone else to grow and move forward in their lives?

I believe that, when we sow generosity, we reap uncountable blessings in this world and the next. My prayer for you, for me, and for everyone whom this book touches is that we never be afraid to share our gifts, and that we always look for new opportunities to give. By doing so, we make room for greater blessings in our own lives.

ASK YOURSELF EACH DAY: "Did I sow any positive seeds today?" List them in the space below.

_____

_____

_____

_____

_____

_____

_____

_____

_____

_____

_____

_____

_____

_____

_____

_____

_____

_____

_____

_____

_____

_____

_____

_____

"Do all the good you can,

By all the means you can,

In all the ways you can,

In all the places you can,

At all the times you can,

To all the people you can,

As long as ever you can."

—JOHN WESLEY

"If you can't feed a hundred people, then just feed one."

—MOTHER TERESA

"What we have done for ourselves alone dies with us; what we have done for others and the world remains and is immortal."

—ALBERT PIKE

SOME FINAL THOUGHTS

Over the course of my life, I have experienced many highs and many lows. One of the most profound lessons I learned from all those ups and down was that it makes absolutely no sense for me to focus on that which I cannot control. I am always better off directing my energy onto the things that I can control.

What this rule means, in a practical sense, is that I was only able to move forward in my life once I decided to stop holding grudges about choices other people had made in the past. These were choices that I felt had affected me adversely, choices I could no longer affect. To move forward in my life, I had to learn to forgive others for making those choices, and I had to acknowledge that I had made my own share of poor choices in life. To move forward in my life, I had to forgive.

As long as there are human beings on this earth, there are going to be conflicts and disagreements about the choices those human beings make in relationship to one another.

Whenever we find ourselves in the midst of adversity or disagreement with another person, we have an important choice to make. Will we choose life, take control of the situation in which we now find ourselves, and become empowered to move forward as a result? Or will we allow resentment, anger, and pain to deplete our resources and drag down our lives?

Will we hold on to past conflicts by looking for reasons to continue them, either out loud or in silence? Or will we begin the process of healing ourselves (and others) by looking for reasons to move past those conflicts?

Forgiveness and gratitude go hand in hand. You cannot be truly grateful when you are holding a grudge. Pay close attention the next time you go through a tough time with regard to your attitude, your choices, the people in your camp, or your own FAITH in

Heal yourself first. Look for a reason to forgive someone. Then act on that reason by finding a way to forgive.

yourself in your mission. What you will notice is that the "tough time" is always accompanied by either a lack of gratitude for the gifts you have been given, or by some lack of forgiveness that connects to a choice someone else made. *Acid burns through the vessel that contains it.* Similarly, a lack of gratitude hurts *you* first ... and worst. A lack of forgiveness hurts *you* first ... and worst.

Down the centuries, lots of people have asked about the secret of true success. Here it is: There is vast power, energy, and creative potential to be found in forgiveness and gratitude.

You will learn this for yourself if you will only follow this simple piece of advice: Before you go to bed each night, ask your Creator to remove all bitterness in your heart toward other people. If you mean it, night after night, and if you live your life in expectation of the fulfillment of that prayer, I believe you will find it very easy to implement the other ideas I have shared with you in this book ... and I believe you will have the power to take the limits off of your life in any area you choose.

"When you hold resentment toward another, you are bound to that person or condition by an emotional link that is stronger than steel. Forgiveness is the only way to dissolve that link and get free."
— CATHERINE PONDER

"There is no love without forgiveness, and there is no forgiveness without love."
— BRYANT H. MCGILL QUOTES

"To forgive is the highest, most beautiful form of love. In return, you will receive untold peace and happiness."
— ROBERT MULLER

"To forgive is to set a prisoner free and discover that the prisoner was you."
— LEWIS B. SMEDES QUOTES

"The weak can never forgive. Forgiveness is the attribute of the strong."
— MAHATMA GANDHI

"Sincere forgiveness isn't colored with expectations that the other person apologize or change. Don't worry whether or not they finally understand you. Love them and release them. Life feeds back truth to people in its own way and time."
— SARA PADDISON

*"To educate yourself for the feeling of gratitude means to take
nothing for granted, but to always seek out and value the kind that
will stand behind the action. Nothing that is done for you is a matter
of course. Everything originates in a will for the good, which is
directed at you. Train yourself never to put off the word or action for
the expression of gratitude."*

—**ALBERT SCHWEITZER**

"Saying thank you is more than good manners. It is good spirituality."

—**ALFRED PAINTER**

*"Gratefulness is the key to a happy life that we hold in our hands,
because if we are not grateful, then no matter how much we have
we will not be happy—because we will always want to have
something else or something more."*

—**BROTHER DAVID STEINDL-RAST**

*"Happiness cannot be traveled to, owned, earned, worn
or consumed. Happiness is the spiritual experience of living
every minute with love, grace and gratitude."*

—**DENIS WAITLEY**

"You say grace before meals. All right. But I say grace before the concert and the opera, and grace before the play and pantomime, and grace before I open a book, and grace before sketching, painting, swimming, fencing, boxing, walking, playing, dancing and grace before I dip the pen in the ink."

—G. K. CHESTERTON

"[D]on't pray when it rains if you don't pray when the sun shines."

—LEROY [SATCHEL] PAIGE

"Appreciation can make a day, even change a life. Your willingness to put it into words is all that is necessary."

—MARGARET COUSINS

"If the only prayer you said in your whole life was, 'thank you,' that would suffice."

—MEISTER ECKHART

Worksheet: Celebrate And Forgive

When was the last time you celebrated progress toward a goal, or the attainment of a goal?

How did you celebrate? With whom?

Is there anyone you hold a grudge against right now? (This could be a family member, a coworker, a client, a current or former boss, or anyone else you feel let you down at some point in your life.)

What would have to happen *internally* for you to forgive that person today? (I'm not asking what you would have to do in order to forget what happened; that's probably impossible. I'm asking what you as a person would have to do, on your own, to reach a point where you no longer held a grudge against this person.)

Appendix A:

THE PRIME OF THEIR LIVES

*S*ometimes people make the mistake of believing that success is a young person's game. Anyone, of any age, can play ... as the following remarkable examples prove. Believe me when I say: If you are forty or older, you have not passed your prime. You have finally *entered* prime time in your life!

Colonel Harland Sanders began franchising restaurants licensed to use his secret recipe for chicken when he was 65.

Rodney Dangerfield worked as an aluminum siding salesman for years before getting his first big break as a comedian when he was 42.

Julia Child did not publish her first cookbook until she was 49, and did not make her television debut until she was in her early fifties.

No Limits!

If you are forty or older, you have not passed your prime. You have finally entered prime time in your life!

The popular Christian writer, speaker, and pastor **Joyce Meyer** did not start her own ministry until she was 42.

Laura Ingalls Wilder published her first book, *Little House in the Big Woods,* when she was 65. It was a huge success; seven sequels followed.

Appendix B:

ON AFFIRMATIONS

Affirmations are phrases or sentences you repeat to support positive changes in the way you look at the world, and at yourself. One of the most famous is the phrase "Every day, in every way, I am getting better and better", which was employed, with astonishing success, by the pioneering hypnotherapist Emile Coue in the early twentieth century.

Affirmations, as the name suggests, affirm and strengthen qualities and abilities the person repeating them wants to make more pronounced in his or her life. It is a tool for more effective, more positive communication with the self. Many people don't concern themselves much with the quality of their self-communication, and this is (I can think of no other word) a tragedy.

The transition I have tried to map out for you in this book -- the transition from a life bound by self-imposed limits to a life in which you really can take the limits off -- is not possible unless you establish and constantly reinforce patterns of positive internal communication. The people I've been privileged to work with who have made the transition I've been writing about in the body of this book, have all learned to see themselves differently, and talk to themselves differently, than they once did.

I know from personal experience that this shift in internal communication takes time and practice, and must be persistently reinforced over time. Frankly, the process of developing a positive habit of seeing and communicating with oneself is so important, and initially so foreign to the many people who attempt to implement it, that it really merits a book of its own. Perhaps someday I'll write such a book. In the meantime, here's a one-sentence summary of my core belief about affirmations:

Affirmations are essential and can work wonders in your life ... but they only work if you have a self-image that is consistent with the affirmations you are repeating.

In other words, we can make whatever changes in our lives we want, as long as we believe, at a deep internal level, that we are capable of making that change. We must find evidence in our lives for the kinds of changes we want our affirmations to help us bring from imagination into reality. If the person we think of as "I" in our own mind's eye is already seen as the kind of person who can overcome virtually any obstacle, then it makes sense, to repeat an affirmation like, "I find new opportunities where others would see only obstacles." On the other hand, if the "I" we are deeply acquainted with is someone we firmly believe is the victim of perpetually unlucky circumstances, then repeating that affirmation will not only be a waste of our time, but also, very likely, confirm the opposite of the worldview we are hoping to reinforce. If the affirmation does not square with our own self-image, it is very likely to do more harm than good.

Dr. Maxwell Maltz, a skilled plastic surgeon, and the author of the book *Psycho-Cybernetics,* was able to confirm this point when tracking the post-surgical experiences of his own patients. After interviewing hundreds of people over a period of years, he concluded that, in any two cases where he had removed a severe facial deformity, it was quite likely that one of the patients would (to use a common phrase) "turn his or her life around" almost immediately -- by, for instance, experiencing dramatic positive changes in his or her career, relationships, or general life outlook. It was just as likely, Maltz concluded, that another patient, one who had undergone the same kind of sudden positive change in physical appearance, would continue to experience major obstacles and challenges in all three of these areas.

How, Maltz asked, could he explain the stark differences between these two common recovery patterns? His answer was, and remains, worthy of close study by all those committed to taking the limits off their own potential for achievement.

The people in the first group already had a generally positive self-image, but saw their facial disfigurement as a temporary obstacle that kept others from perceiving them as they really were. The moment that that obstacle was removed, they saw themselves as free to pursue their goals, and attain those goals. *They now believed that they were capable of success, and that they deserved to succeed.*

The people in the second group presented a very different world view. They had internalized, bought into, personalized, an image of themselves as "not okay," a self-image that their physical deformity had not created, but had only served, over the years, to confirm. When the facial deformity was removed, many of them insisted that the problem remained, despite ample physical evidence to the contrary, and despite the pleas of friends, relatives, and Dr. Maltz himself to notice the seemingly obvious changes for the better by consulting the nearest mirror. For these patients, the image in the mirror on the wall was irrelevant. What mattered was the image they held of themselves in the mirror of their own minds. There, they were still disfigured, and would remain so until they themselves changed the picture. Dr. Maltz concluded that no amount of "positive thinking" would change the life experience of these patients ... not, at least, until they made a conscious choice to take part in a DAILY campaign to change their own self-image. Until that happened, they were prisoners of their own self-limiting beliefs. *They did not believe that they were capable of success, or that they deserved to succeed.* So the old patterns persisted.

The obvious question at this point is: HOW DOES ONE CHANGE THE INTERNAL PICTURE? And the answer Maltz offered, which is identical to the answer offered by Emile Coue half a century earlier, is a simple one:

Combine spoken or silent affirmations with intense visualizations that offer your brain clear proof of the content of the affirmation. Then continue this practice daily for a period of weeks or even months. The best time to do this is right before you go to sleep at night.

So for instance: If the affirmation you choose is, "I find opprtunities where others would see only obstacles," don't just repeat those words emptily to yourself a dozen or so times as you drive to work in the morning. Wait for the evening. As you get into bed, take a few moments to shield yourself from all distractions, then close your eyes and PICTURE a time when you actually did find opportunity in apparent adversity. Feel the good feelings you felt when you did this. Repeat the affirmation to yourself with deep emotion, either silently or out loud. Next, picture yourself in some future setting, finding opportunity where others would find only obstacles. Be as specific as you can. Feel all the good feelings. Repeat your affirmation.

The process I'm describing will take only a few minutes each night. It will not deliver instant results. But if you keep it up persistently, night after night, for perhaps sixty days, I believe that you will find that your internal communication skills improve over that time, that your self-image becomes more positive, and that you will find it easier to take the limits off in your own life.

Below, you will find a list of some of my favorite affirmations. Use these, or use affirmations of your own choosing—but be sure you use them as part of a DAILY process in which you SEE yourself improving, in your own mind's eye.

Keep your affirmations positive!

✦ I am grateful for all that is good in my life.

✦ I love how I find opportunities where others would see only obstacles.

✦ I love that I easily attract the best in people.

✦ I love how other people are experiencing this positive energy I am feeling.

✦ I love how all things are possible.

✦ I take appropriate action.

✦ I am loved and appreciated, and I love and appreciate others.

✦ I've got the time needed to do what matters to me.

✦ Money comes quickly and easily to me.

✦ I am healthy and energized to do all that I choose to do.

About the Author

A dynamic professional speaker and coach, Joyce Dungee Proctor offers a wealth of practical strategies to empower and challenge her audiences. Joyce's mission is to inspire you to "Take the Limits Off" to achieve your purpose and fulfill your dreams.

Joyce's engaging, energizing style and her ability to connect with her audiences by sharing real life experiences serves as catalysts to inspire you to move beyond contemplating change and make the changes necessary to take your life and career to the next level.

Joyce has over 20 years of leadership, business management, training, and human resources experience. She is the President of Seminars by Joyce–The Total You, Inc. specializing in keynotes, seminars, and workshops that are customized and designed to meet the unique needs of each client and audience. Joyce's presentations are thought-provoking, solutions-oriented, and highly interactive, offering techniques and valuable resources to drive immediate application and results!

For more information, and to book Joyce to speak at your next event, please visit www.seminarsbyjoyce.com or call 302-438-8478.
www.takethelimitsoffevents.com

To purchase additional copies of this book go to
my websites or Amazon.com.

A Note From My Mentor

$\mathcal{J}$oyce is an inspiration to those of us who have been stuck in the same place year after year – with our lives, our careers, and our businesses. With her book you can finally "take the limits off" because Joyce inspires us with her own story, gives practical advice and the tools needed to get started right away- Today. The exercises, anecdotes, quotes and Joyce's own personal journey combine to make a practical handbook for anyone aspiring to do something different with their life-Now! This is not just a book to read and set aside; it is a tool to allow you to "take the limits off" that provides a template that when used, can become YOUR PERSONAL PLAN- Right Away. Keep this book with you and use regularly and you will see the fruit grow from the seeds you plant.

Through this effort, Joyce shared with me that I inspired her to strike out on her own as an independent business woman, something I did 20 years ago. As a business performance consultant, I am excited when I see resources that encourage people to plan positively, think affirmatively, live with purpose and achieve results. This work accomplishes all of this and more! I am honored that I have been an inspiration to her. She has truly inspired me as well by sharing her desires and dreams for her business. I admire her for her tenacity, her commitment, "stick-to-it-ness", and her ability to love and give. She does all of this with passion and the same degree of excellence she exhibits when offering her "seminars by Joyce" and in her speaking. She is a perfect example of how planting seeds with all people, sharing her spirit of positive energy and extending love to others works it's way back seven fold. To Joyce: congratulations on the success of your first book. Thanks for sharing who you are and what you know with the world. It's electric!

DEVONA E. G.WILLIAMS, PH.D.

PRESIDENT/CEO

GOEINS-WILLIAMS ASSOCIATES, INC.

PERFORMANCE CONSULTING

CLAYTON, DELAWARE